St Peter and the Holy and
Indivisible Trinity

# A Welcome from The Dean

Welcome to Gloucester Cathedral!
This exquisitely beautiful structure was
built as a place of prayer to God and as a
place of Christian pilgrimage. I hope that
you will enjoy your visit here and you will
see it, too, as a pilgrimage. I invite you
most warmly to say your prayers here,
either quietly in one of the chapels by
yourself or by joining our daily worship.
Prayers have been offered here for over
thirteen hundred years.

   Only the very best is good enough for
God and that is why the cathedral was built
of the best materials and is continually
being restored in the traditional way.
Gloucestershire people are enormously
proud of this stunningly lovely building
but we are equally proud of our reputation
for being one of the friendliest cathedrals
in Britain. I very much hope that you will
find a warm welcome, and may you leave
this place refreshed and uplifted. May God
bless you on your journey.

A t every stage of the cathedral's history, one activity stands out from the huge variety of things that happen here – worship. When Gloucester Abbey became a cathedral in 1541, the statutes of King Henry VIII laid down that it was for 'the pure worship of God to flourish and the holy Gospel of Christ to be diligently preached'. From 1089 the abbey community had prayer at the heart of its life, coming together seven times a day for prayer and the celebration of the Mass.

Nine hundred years later, worship is still the foundation of the life of the cathedral. Every day of the year Holy Communion is celebrated, often with the choir singing. Prayers are offered each morning and evening, a special element here being those requested by people coming to the cathedral. Candles are lit so that others may share in the prayers and be heartened by the sign of Jesus Christ as the light of the world.

Large groups come here for ordinations, carol services, public commemorations and great celebrations. Baptisms and weddings take place, but perhaps fewer than one might expect, as the number of people who actually live around the cathedral is small.

On your visit you may find the building in one of many moods: almost empty with the sound of voices in the distance when there is a service in progress; so crowded that no more people can get in; the vergers may be working to keep it clean for the thousands who enter each week; masons may be repairing the stone; organ tuners may be at work.

Whatever is happening, the cathedral is here for the praise and worship of God and for people to find a place to pray as they have done for centuries past.

*ABOVE: Sunday morning worship in the quire.* ⑫

ABOVE: *To light a candle can be a powerful and comforting expression of prayer when words prove hard to find.*

*BELOW: A service of baptism in the Lady Chapel, using the ancaut font.* ⑰

*ABOVE: A window (1901) by Christopher Whall in the Lady Chapel, depicting the Nativity of Jesus Christ.* ⑰

In 678–9 King Ethelred of Mercia assigned to Osric, prince in the province of the Hwicce, an area of land within the former Roman town of Glevum for the building of a religious house dedicated to St Peter. Thought to have been headed by Abbess Cyneburgh, the community consisted of royal and noble widows and had facilities for educating their children; resident priests would say Mass. In the later 8th century, the house became a college of secular priests; in the early 11th century, Bishop Wulfstan of Worcester installed Benedictine monks. Bishop Ealdred enlarged the abbey in 1058. Nothing now remains of this Anglo-Saxon monastery.

In 1072, William the Conqueror appointed Serlo, a Norman monk from Mont-Saint-Michel, as Abbot of Gloucester. Serlo revitalized the abbey, expanding the number of monks and increasing the income from the extensive estates. By the time of Domesday in 1086, assets were double their pre-1066 level and Serlo therefore set about building a new abbey in the Romanesque style. This was consecrated in 1100 although work still continued on the nave and some domestic buildings.

Greater income resulted in several ambitious building projects: a central tower (1222), the first Lady Chapel (1228), the nave vault (1242), a south-west tower (after 1243), and a refectory (1246). Popular devotion to the deposed King Edward II, buried at Gloucester, generated the money in the mid-14th century for the remodelling of the south transept, the quire and east window, the north transept and the cloisters. In the 15th century, Abbot Morwent pulled down the Norman west end and rebuilt it, adding the south porch. Abbot Sebrok began building the present tower in 1450, and Abbot Hanley the present Lady Chapel c.1470.

ABOVE: *An effigy of Serlo, who began the building of the new Norman abbey in the last years of the 11th century.* ⑬

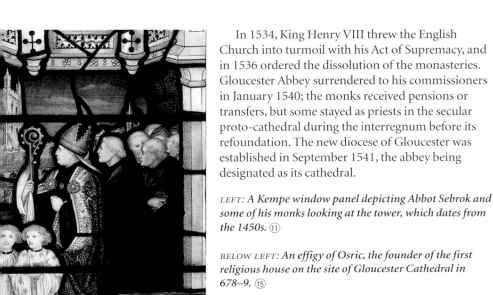

In 1534, King Henry VIII threw the English Church into turmoil with his Act of Supremacy, and in 1536 ordered the dissolution of the monasteries. Gloucester Abbey surrendered to his commissioners in January 1540; the monks received pensions or transfers, but some stayed as priests in the secular proto-cathedral during the interregnum before its refoundation. The new diocese of Gloucester was established in September 1541, the abbey being designated as its cathedral.

LEFT: *A Kempe window panel depicting Abbot Sebrok and some of his monks looking at the tower, which dates from the 1450s.* ⑪

BELOW LEFT: *An effigy of Osric, the founder of the first religious house on the site of Gloucester Cathedral in 678–9.* ⑮

ABOVE: *A window panel (1892) by Charles Kempe showing Serlo with two French noblewomen and two monks in the nave of his new abbey.* ⑪

Serlo's spacious nave dates from the end of the 11th century, and is an outstanding example of Romanesque building. Vast cylindrical Norman columns (almost 10 metres [32 feet] in height and 2 metres [6 feet] in diameter) carry an arcade of narrow arches to the height of the normal triforium, the style derived from Tournus Abbey in Burgundy. Above the arcade Serlo planned a reduced triforium and a clerestory, altered in later rebuilding. Repair work culminated in the Early English rib vault added in 1242. Originally, the Norman nave was about 5 metres (16 feet) longer than it is now, with twin towers at the west end, one of which collapsed in the late 13th century. During the 1420s, Abbot Morwent rebuilt the two most westerly bays in the Perpendicular style and added the south porch.

Serlo's north aisle retains its Norman rib-vault, but in 1318 Abbot Toky remodelled the south aisle to prevent subsidence, incorporating ballflower decoration on the vault in the three eastern bays.

King Henry III had his first coronation in Gloucester Abbey on 28 October 1216. A Victorian window in the south aisle depicts the young king flanked by the Pope's representative, Cardinal Guala Bicchieri, and Peter des Roches, the Bishop of Winchester, who performed the ceremony.

HENRICVS · REX · IN · ECCLESIA · GLOVCESTRIE · CO

ABOVE: *The first coronation of King Henry III at Gloucester; a window of 1860 by Clayton & Bell.* ㉔

OPPOSITE: *The nave, looking east, with its massive Norman columns and its Early English roof vault, dating from 1242.* ③

BELOW: *Ballflower decoration in the south aisle; the embellishment is found only in this region of England.* ㉔

RIGHT:
*The themes of the west window (Wailes, 1859) are the birth of Christ and the doctrine of baptism.* ③

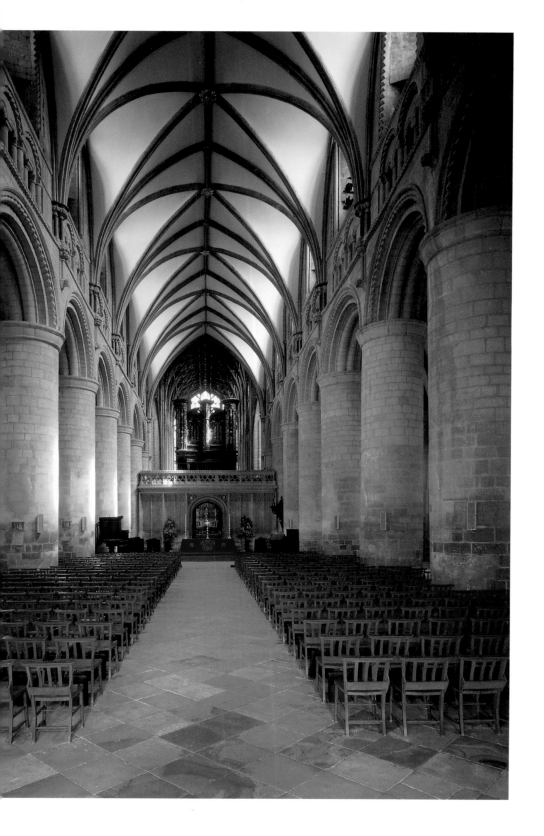

It was the offerings of pilgrims to the tomb of King Edward II that helped Abbot Adam de Staunton's architects to transform Serlo's dark Romanesque quire between 1337 and 1348 into the present Perpendicular quire. This he did by constructing a stone screen on the inside surface of the original Norman arcade. Then he removed the roof, pulled down the apse at the east end, and proceeded to carry the screen walls (pierced by tall windows) up to a new height, building upon them a magnificent lierne vault which is 27 metres (88 feet) above the floor. In place of the apse, he designed a

ABOVE: *The door in the quire ceiling through which bells are raised and lowered to and from the tower.* ⑫

rectangular east end to contain the largest stained-glass window in the country. New stalls for the monks occupied the north and south sides; of the 58 misericords, 44 are medieval while the others are Victorian. On the south side near the presbytery is the Bishop's throne; it is the fact that the Bishop of Gloucester has his seat in this building (the Greek word for seat is *kathedra*) which gives the cathedral its title.

Moving east, the presbytery leads to the sanctuary, where is preserved the encaustic tiled pavement laid by Abbot Sebrok in 1455. On the vault above the high altar is the central figure of Christ in glory surrounded by bosses of angels playing musical instruments. The present high altar and reredos were designed by Sir George Gilbert Scott and dedicated in 1873.

ABOVE: *A corner of the quire showing the Dean's stall.* ⑫

OPPOSITE: *The quire looking west.* ⑫

ABOVE: *A misericord showing an elephant. These 'mercy' seats allowed elderly or infirm monks to sit while appearing to stand. The elephant may well have been carved from someone's oral description.* ⑫

Gloucester's great east window is the largest window in terms of overall area in any medieval cathedral around Britain. It measures 22 metres (72 feet) in height and 12 metres (38 feet) in width; to encompass this vast expanse of glass, the quire widens at its extreme east end.

Assembled during the 1350s, the colourful glass reflects the hierarchical nature of medieval society as well as the Church's interpretation of Divine Order; for the medieval monks, this window was in practice a massive glass reredos above the high altar.

Its centrepiece is the coronation of the Blessed Virgin Mary who sits with our Lord Jesus Christ flanked by the 12 apostles, six on each side. In the tier below are pairs of saints and martyrs, female and male, and in the next tier are Abbots of Gloucester and Bishops of Worcester. Coats of arms appear in the lowest tier including those of King Edward II, King Edward III, Lord Thomas Bradeston and Sir Maurice Berkeley. Over the six centuries of its existence, the great window survived all the vicissitudes of history and remains in good condition. Re-leading and cleaning of the glass took place in the 1860s, and the window underwent further conservation in 1976–7 and 1998–9.

ABOVE: *A detail from the east window, depicting Jesus Christ, his hand raised in blessing his mother.* ⑭

ABOVE: *A further detail from the window, showing the Coronation of the Blessed Virgin Mary.* ⑭

LEFT: *Stonemasons at work on the restoration of the tracery.*

OPPOSITE: *The window, with its large expanse of colourful medieval glass.* ⑭

The south transept of Gloucester Cathedral represents the first full flowering of the Perpendicular style of English architecture. As with the quire, the money from pilgrims to the tomb of King Edward II enabled Abbot Wygemor to finance the remodelling of the original Norman transept during the 1330s; on its east side, the Perpendicular panelling is threaded by the flying buttresses of the tower. Moving from the nave into the south transept, on the north side is a chantry chapel containing the tomb of Abbot Sebrok, who initiated the rebuilding of the tower in 1450. Next on the north side is St John the Baptist's Chapel with its wooden parclose screen dating from the middle of the 16th century. On the east side is St Andrew's Chapel redecorated by Gambier Parry (who lived locally) in 1868 and restored in 1996. Near the entrance to the crypt is the Prentice bracket commemorating an anonymous young stonemason who fell to his death while working on the building of the abbey.

As with the south transept, the north transept received its Perpendicular veneer between 1368 and 1373 but with more accomplished lierne vaulting than its counterpart. On the east side is St Paul's Chapel which retains its original Romanesque form. Along the north side, the veranda screen functions as the entrance to the Treasury which occupies the east slype, once a passage from the cloister walk to the monastic cemetery. Against the west wall, above the monument to the Bower family, is a clock designed in 1903 by Henry Wilson in memory of Bartholomew Price, a residentiary canon of the cathedral.

ABOVE: *St Andrew's Chapel in the south transept is elaborately decorated in high Victorian neo-Gothic style.* ㉑

LEFT: *The tomb effigy of Thomas Sebrok, Abbot 1450–57, who began the rebuilding of the tower.* ㉓

ABOVE: *A clock (1903) made by Henry Wilson. Its design reflects Bartholomew Price's interest in astronomy; the hours are portrayed by bronze medallions showing the signs of the zodiac.* ⑧

ABOVE: *A detail from St Andrew's Chapel, painted by Gambier Parry, the father of Sir Hubert Parry, famous composer of religious music.* ㉑

ABOVE: *The Prentice bracket in the south transept commemorates the death of an apprentice mason while he was working on the building of the abbey.* ⑳

13

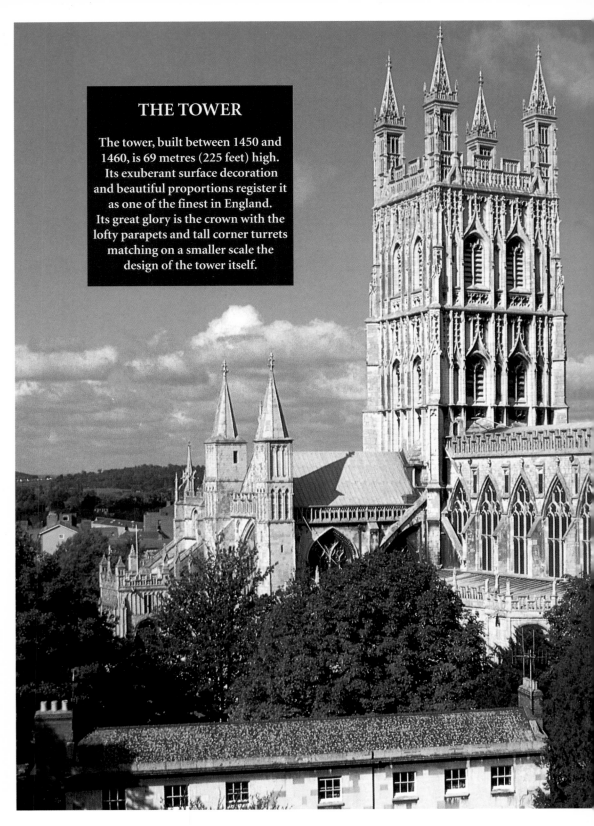

# THE TOWER

The tower, built between 1450 and 1460, is 69 metres (225 feet) high. Its exuberant surface decoration and beautiful proportions register it as one of the finest in England. Its great glory is the crown with the lofty parapets and tall corner turrets matching on a smaller scale the design of the tower itself.

# THE BELLS

Since 1460 the bells have been augmented in stages to twelve. Several were cast locally by the Rudhall family. In addition to the twelve hung for change ringing, another bell, Great Peter, is the only medieval Bourdon bell remaining in England. Weighing over 59cwt, its majestic deep tone marks the daylight hours for the city.

Both sides of the ambulatory around the quire date from the last decade of the 11th century, and remain as Serlo's architect designed them: three radiating chapels (including the west end of the present Lady Chapel) form a chevet which repeats itself in the crypt below and in the tribune gallery above.

In the south ambulatory is the effigy of Robert, Duke of Normandy, eldest son of William the Conqueror. Robert became embroiled in a struggle for succession with his brother, King Henry I, who imprisoned him in 1106. Robert died in captivity at Cardiff Castle in 1134 and was buried in Gloucester's Chapter House. His effigy was made a century or so later from Irish bog oak, and is probably a tribute from some warriors of the third crusade to the memory of the hero of the first crusade; it reclines on a 15th-century tomb chest. Opposite the effigy are two remarkable 15th-century cope chests which used to contain the medieval ecclesiastical vestments.

Reordering of the South Ambulatory Chapel took place in 1989; the middle light of the new window shows Christ appearing to Thomas, while the outer lights interpret Psalm 148. In the North Ambulatory Chapel, windows commemorate the fallen from the Gloucestershire Regiment in the Korean War, while memorial books record the names of those from the Gloucester diocese who died in both World Wars.

ABOVE: *A window (1892) by Kempe depicting Abbot Wygemor with King Edward III near the tomb of the king's father in the early 1330s.* ⑪

Along the north ambulatory are three tombs: the first is a Tudor tomb to Osric, the founder of the first religious house. Another chantry is to William Malvern (known also as Parker), the last Abbot of Gloucester who disappeared in 1539. The centrepiece is the splendid tomb of King Edward II who died while imprisoned at Berkeley Castle in September 1327; his effigy is made of alabaster and rests on a tomb chest of oolitic limestone clad in Purbeck marble. Despite Edward's woeful performance as a monarch, English respect for the divine right of kings made his tomb at Gloucester a place of veneration for thousands of medieval pilgrims.

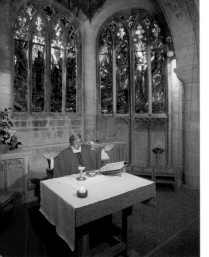

ABOVE: *The celebration of Holy Communion in the South Ambulatory Chapel.* ⑱

RIGHT: *The effigy of Robert, Duke of Normandy, eldest son of William the Conqueror. He died in 1134 at Cardiff Castle, a prisoner of his younger brother, King Henry I.* ⑲

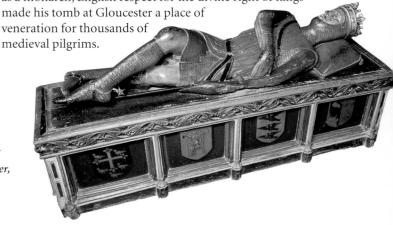

16

ABOVE: *The tomb of King Edward II. The deposed ruler was buried on the north side of the presbytery in December 1327.* ⑪

RIGHT: *A detail of the tomb showing the face of the king's effigy.* ⑪

Leading off the ambulatory at the east end is the Lady Chapel, which represents the final flowering of the Perpendicular style of English architecture; its construction resembles that of King's College, Cambridge, that is to say, a vaulted roof supported on a series of stone arches filled with tall stained-glass windows. These were made by the famous 'Arts and Crafts' artist Christopher Whall in the early 1900s, and are some of the finest post-medieval windows in the country. Begun around 1470 and finished about 20 years later, it is the third and largest chapel to stand on this site, replacing the earlier Norman apse.

Situated near the west end, the Norman lead font, dating from about 1130, came from Lancaut church in the Wye Valley. In front of the altar are the wooden communion rails made in 1617 on the orders of Dean William Laud. The reredos sustained serious damage in 1643 at the hands of Cromwell's Parliamentarians during the English Civil War.

Occupying the North Chantry Chapel is the colourful effigy of Godfrey Goldsborough who was Bishop of Gloucester from 1598 to 1604; the South Chantry Chapel contains stained-glass windows in memory of four Gloucester organists (S.S. Wesley, C.H. Lloyd, Herbert Brewer and Herbert Sumsion) along with the composer Herbert Howells.

ABOVE: *A window by Christopher Whall (1909). An angel combines the blue of the cherubim with the red of the seraphim.* ⑰

RIGHT: *The Lady Chapel looking west, showing the tribune gallery.* ⑰

OPPOSITE: *The Lady Chapel looking east.* ⑰

OPPOSITE INSET: *An effigy of Bishop Goldsborough from the north chantry of the Lady Chapel.* ⑰

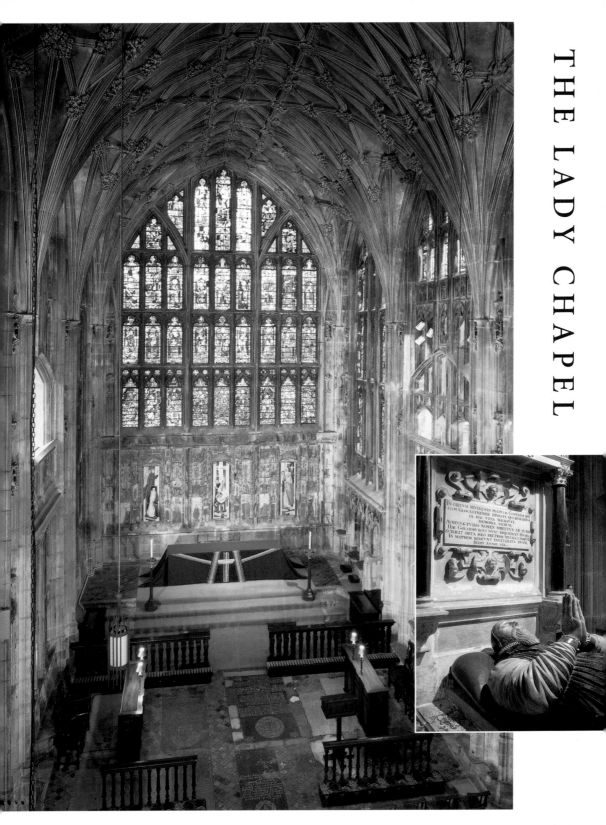

Gloucester's great cloister is famous for the magnificent fan vaulting which can be seen above all four of its walks. The cloister was an enclosed place in the monastery where monks worked, taught, walked and meditated. In most abbeys it was situated on the warmer south side of the church, but Gloucester's cloister lies unusually to the north. Its layout follows the normal Benedictine plan whereby all the domestic buildings branched off the cloister walks.

Begun in the latter part of the 14th century and finished by Abbot Froucester before 1412, it replaced the narrower Norman cloister. Froucester's design incorporated a row of 20 carrels along the south walk; each of these had a wooden desk where the monks sat for study. Along the west end of the north walk, the washing place (*lavatorium*) extends into the cloister garth, and made use of a stream called the Fullbrook. Through their daily round of services, the monks used the east walk to process via the north transept into the quire.

In the centre of the east walk of the cloister is the Chapter House, constructed by Abbot Serlo in 1085. It was used by the monks of Gloucester for formal assemblies and the transaction of the daily business of the abbey. The Chapter House consists of three Norman bays, with a 15th-century eastern bay and window replacing the original Norman apse. Robert, Duke of Normandy, is buried here along with several other benefactors of St Peter's Abbey in the early 12th century.

*ABOVE: The* lavatorium *in the north walk of the cloister, where monks used to wash themselves, is the finest example in Britain.* ㉗

*LEFT: The west walk of the cloister. Unusually Gloucester's cloisters are on the north side of the church.* ㉕

*ABOVE: An inscription to Robert, Duke of Normandy on the south arcade of the Chapter House.* ㉘

21

As the mother church of the diocese, the cathedral contains memorials not only to bishops, deans and residentiary canons, but also to many other people from all walks of life around Gloucestershire, famous and not so famous. In recent years, the skill and sensitivity of Ivor Gurney (died 1937) as a poet and songwriter, who together with Herbert Howells gave the beauty of Gloucestershire expression in music, has been rediscovered by a new generation.

IN MEMORY OF
JOHN STAFFORD SMITH
1750-1836 who, born in this city, son of Martin Smith organist of the Cathedral 1743-1782, was a composer of distinction, a well-known musical antiquary, and organist of the Chapel Royal London. He will long be remembered as composer of the tune of the National Anthem of the United States of America

ABOVE: *A memorial to John Stafford Smith (1750–1836), composer of the American National Anthem.* ⑦

IVOR
GURNEY
1890-1937

composer
and
poet
chorister
of this
Cathedral
Church

Do not forget
me quite
O Severn
meadows

ABOVE: *A wall plaque from the north aisle commemorating Ivor Gurney.* ⑥

ABOVE: *The family monument in the north aisle of Thomas Machen (died 1614), his wife and children.* ⑤

22

Some memorials are plain ledger stones in the floor, while others constitute some of the cathedral's finest works of art. Two contrasting examples can be seen in the monument to the Machen family and their 13 children, erected in 1614, next to which is an exquisite bronze of a kneeling priest, designed in 1897 by Henry Wilson in memory of Canon Edward Tinling. Wilson's art nouveau chalice, also for Canon Tinling, is in the cathedral treasury.

JENNER

ABOVE: *A statue of Edward Jenner (1749–1823), the pioneer of vaccination, who was born and practised at Berkeley.* ②

ABOVE: *Edward Tinling was from 1867 to 1897 a canon of the cathedral. A chalice in the treasury (pictured overleaf) and this bronze in the north aisle commemorate him.* ⑤

Thanks to the generosity of the Worshipful Company of Goldsmiths in London, the cathedral treasury (situated off the north transept) was opened in 1977 and contains a splendid display of silver plate from the 15th century onwards. As well as items from churches around the diocese, there is a fine set of vessels for the Holy Communion used in the cathedral after the restoration of the monarchy in 1660.

*ABOVE: The cross used regularly for processions during services.* ⑪

*RIGHT: Two items from the treasury: a Restoration flagon and the Tinling chalice.* ⑨

Steps from the south transept lead to the crypt, which extends beneath the presbytery and beyond. Only here does Serlo's original apse survive intact, dating from around 1087. The centre portion is encircled with an ambulatory, the vault of which springs from small piers and is supported on outer walls 2.5 metres (8 feet) thick. The weight of the quire proved too much for the piers, which were strengthened with additional arches and ribs *c.*1100. In the 14th century the quire was heightened, and two huge shapeless piers at the east end of the crypt were added to carry the increased weight.

An important enhancement of Christian worship in the Church of England is the cathedral tradition of choral music, continuing at Gloucester the practice of the medieval monks of St Peter's Abbey. In accordance with King Henry VIII's statutes of 1544, all the cathedral choristers receive their academic education at The King's School. Nowadays, the men of the choir, known as lay clerks, follow independent careers. The choir sings the Sunday services and daily Evensong, embracing a wide repertoire of music by composers from the last 500 years. Also, the choir visits various churches around the diocese, goes abroad on tour, and has made a number of acclaimed recordings of religious music.

Central to this tradition of cathedral music is the use of the organ to accompany services and anthems, and also to act as a solo instrument playing voluntaries before and after the main services and improvisation within the liturgy. Gloucester's versatile organ incorporates the original decorated pipework on its east (Front Great) and west faces from the 1665 Thomas Harris instrument, which underwent careful restoration in the 1971 rebuild. Originally on the south side of the quire, the organ assumed its present position on the screen in the early 18th century.

ABOVE: *Two panels from the window in the south chantry celebrating the church music of Herbert Howells (1892–1983). It was designed by Caroline Swash in 1992 to mark the centenary of the composer's birth in Gloucestershire, and portrays music from four of his anthems.* (17)

LEFT: *The stone plaque at the end of the south aisle (west wall) is in memory of the composer Hubert Parry (1848–1918) who was born near Gloucester. Designed by Emery Walker, and unveiled during the Three Choirs Festival in September 1922, it bears an inscription by Robert Bridges who was Poet Laureate at the time.*

ABOVE: *The eastern prospect of the cathedral organ, showing the Front Great organ case designed by Thomas Harris in 1665, along with the smaller Chaire case built by Thomas Dallam around 1640.* ⑫

With over thirteen hundred years of Christian worship and life on the same spot, there is a deep feeling of rooted spirituality which not only connects us to the past, but also gives us strength for today and inspiration to continue our journey into the future. This magnificent cathedral is our inheritance, and we strive to maintain it stone by stone for generations to come; we have our own skilled workers including masons, carpenters and other staff.

Far more than a stone monument, the cathedral is a community of people and a living church where worship takes place every day. Clergy, choir, organists, vergers, congregation and Children's Church follow the cathedral's daily pattern; visiting choirs and various groups play their part also.

Volunteer guides, welcomers, cleaners, flower arrangers and many others give their time freely to make the cathedral what it is today. Whether you would like a guided tour or to be left in peace, our staff and volunteers are here to help you enjoy your visit.

ABOVE: *A flower arranger prepares the display for the Sunday services.*

CENTRE: *A verger prepares for a service in St John's Chapel in the south transept.*

RIGHT: *A member of the cathedral's cleaning team polishes the brass lectern in the quire.*

## HISTORY CHART

| | |
|---|---|
| 678–9 | Osric establishes first religious house. |
| 1017 | Benedictine monks in residence. |
| 1072 | William I appoints Serlo as Abbot. |
| 1089 | Foundation stone laid for Serlo's abbey. |
| 1100 | Consecration of St Peter's Abbey. |
| 1216 | First coronation of King Henry III. |
| 1327 | Burial of King Edward II. |
| 1331 | Perpendicular remodelling of the quire. |
| 1373 | Cloisters begun by Abbot Horton. |
| 1420 | West end rebuilt by Abbot Morwent. |
| 1450 | Tower begun by Abbot Sebrok. |
| 1470 | Lady Chapel rebuilt. |
| 1540 | Dissolution of abbey. |
| 1541 | King Henry VIII establishes cathedral. |
| 1616 | James I appoints William Laud as Dean. |
| 1649 | Abolition of Dean and Chapter. |
| 1660 | Charles II reinstates Dean and Chapter. |
| 1735 | Bishop Benson undertakes structural alterations. |
| 1873 | Refurbishment by Sir George Gilbert Scott finished. |
| 1989 | 900th anniversary appeal. |
| 1994 | Restoration of tower completed. |
| 2003 | Maundy service attended by Her Majesty The Queen. |

## VISIT THE GLOUCESTER CATHEDRAL WEBSITE!

www.gloucestercathedral.org.uk

*ABOVE: Choral Evensong is an unforgettable experience. All are welcome to attend.* ⑫

Acknowledgements

The publishers wish to acknowledge the kind assistance of the Revd. Judith Hubbard-Jones and Lowinger Maddison in the preparation of this book.

The text was written by Lowinger Maddison.
Edited by John McIlwain.
Designed by Tim Noel-Johnson.
The photographs are © Jarrold Publishing (by Peter Smith of Newbery Smith Photography and Mark Fiennes) except for Jack Farley: pp 3 (all), 6 (top right), 8, 10 (right, top and bottom), 18 (left), 28 (all); Gloucester Cathedral (by Alison Liddle): inside front cover–p 1; R.W. Rudge ABIPP: front cover, pp 14–15; R.J.L. Smith of Much Wenlock: p 11.

Text © Gloucester Cathedral.

Publication in this form © Jarrold Publishing 1999, latest reprint 2004.

No part of this publication may be reproduced by any means without the permission of Jarrold Publishing and the copyright holders.

Pitkin Guides is an imprint of Jarrold Publishing, Norwich.

Printed in Great Britain.
ISBN 0 85372 962 X          3/04

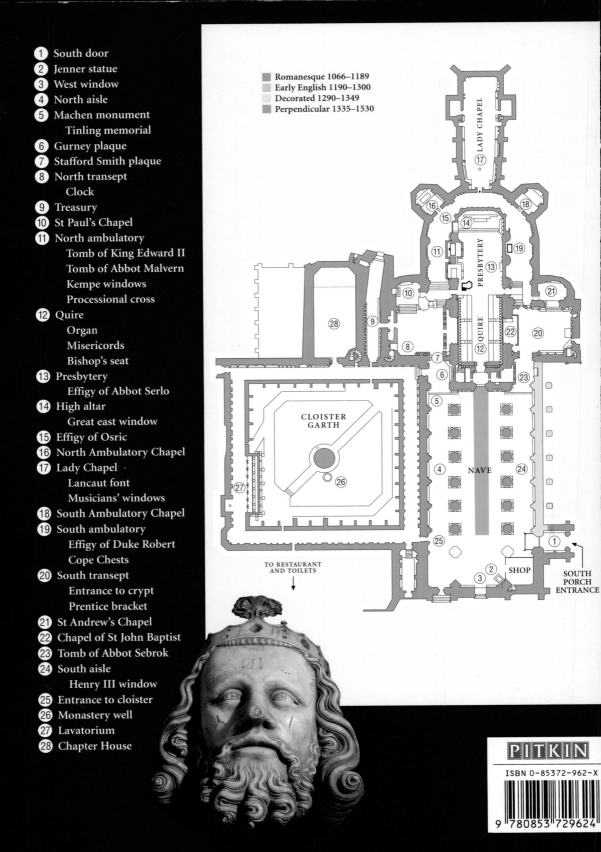

1. South door
2. Jenner statue
3. West window
4. North aisle
5. Machen monument
   Tinling memorial
6. Gurney plaque
7. Stafford Smith plaque
8. North transept
   Clock
9. Treasury
10. St Paul's Chapel
11. North ambulatory
    Tomb of King Edward II
    Tomb of Abbot Malvern
    Kempe windows
    Processional cross
12. Quire
    Organ
    Misericords
    Bishop's seat
13. Presbytery
    Effigy of Abbot Serlo
14. High altar
    Great east window
15. Effigy of Osric
16. North Ambulatory Chapel
17. Lady Chapel ·
    Lancaut font
    Musicians' windows
18. South Ambulatory Chapel
19. South ambulatory
    Effigy of Duke Robert
    Cope Chests
20. South transept
    Entrance to crypt
    Prentice bracket
21. St Andrew's Chapel
22. Chapel of St John Baptist
23. Tomb of Abbot Sebrok
24. South aisle
    Henry III window
25. Entrance to cloister
26. Monastery well
27. Lavatorium
28. Chapter House

Romanesque 1066–1189
Early English 1190–1300
Decorated 1290–1349
Perpendicular 1335–1530

LADY CHAPEL

PRESBYTERY

QUIRE

CLOISTER GARTH

NAVE

TO RESTAURANT
AND TOILETS

SHOP

SOUTH
PORCH
ENTRANCE

PITKIN
ISBN 0-85372-962-X
9 780853 729624